C000048775

A BOOT UP

SALISBURY PLAIN

Rodney Legg

First published in Great Britain in 2009

British Library Cataloguing-in-Publication Data
A CIP record for this title is available from the British Library

ISBN 978 1 906887 11 7

PiXZ Books
Halsgrove House, Ryelands Industrial Estate,
Bagley Road, Wellington, Somerset TA21 9PZ
Tel: 01823 653777
Fax: 01823 216796
email: sales@halsgrove.com

An imprint of Halstar Ltd, part of the Halsgrove group of companies
Information on all Halsgrove titles is available at: www.halsgrove.com

Printed and bound by Grafiche Flaminia, Italy

Contents

Salisbury Plain

How to use this book

The Area

These walks are beside, and sometimes inside, DTE SP. The initials stand for Defence Training Estate Salisbury Plain. This comprises Britain's biggest military firing ranges, which is more intensively used than ever since the end of the Cold War, because of the repatriation from Germany of the British Army of the Rhine.

This is the largest natural chalkland landscape in Britain and Europe. Because of military presence, much of the area escaped the agricultural revolution, and remains as a single immense expanse of virgin downland which has been unploughed since prehistory. Some 80 square miles - more than 50,000 acres - have been designated as SSSI (Site of Special Scientific Interest) by Natural England.

Scattered across it are hundreds of ancient burial mounds and the humps and hollows of numerous settlements from the past 6,000 years. Around its edges, Salisbury Plain is ringed by major Wessex hill-forts, a collection of chalk-cut horses, and the World Heritage Site of Stonehenge and Avebury.

Army requirements and weapons will inevitably change, with the result that present paths and routes may be subject to closure or rationalisation. Lieutenant-Colonel Mike Beard describes this as 'a difficult balance between the needs of military training, safety and public access'.

The Routes

All routes are circular - meaning they bring you back to the starting point - and are of moderate length. They vary from four to eight miles and are graded from one to three boots - from easy to the more challenging. They are ideal for families or groups of friends looking for an afternoon in glorious historic countryside or for a more leisurely walk with a suitable pause at a pub or refreshment spot en route. None of the terrain is pushchair friendly, so back-pack the toddler.

Starting points are given with map references and postcodes, because the latter are necessary for some car-borne navigation systems, including that used by an ambulance crew who told me they were 15 minutes late in arriving at an emergency because no postcode was given.

Direction details specify compass points which, clockwise, are N (north), NNE (north-northeast), E (east), ESE (east-southeast), SE (south-east), SSE (south-southeast), S (south), SSW (south-southwest), SW (south-west), WSW (west-southwest), W (west), WNW (west-northwest), NW (north-west) and WNW (west-northwest). The general direction can be assumed to remain the same until another compass point is given. Carry a compass.

Routes are along public rights of way or across access land. Both categories may be subject to change or diversion. Some inside Ministry of Defence land will be subject to bylaws and restrictions. Remember that conditions under foot will vary greatly according to the season and the weather. Do not set off into the hills if fog is present or likely.

Parking spaces are specified on the assumption that many walkers will arrive by car or bicycle. Where public transport is mentioned, there were options currently available, but check these with the provider before setting off and always make sure you also know the time of the last bus or train.

The Maps

Though we give a self-contained potted description of each walk you may need a map or global positioning system to find its parking point. Our sketch maps can only be a rough guide. A detailed map will prove useful if you stray from the route or are forced to cut the walk short. Remember that practical difficulties on the day may range from exhaustion to hill fog.

Two large-scale Ordnance Survey maps currently cover Salisbury plain. These are Explorer 130 (Salisbury & Stonehenge) and 143 (Warminster & Trowbridge). For availability, access www.ordnancesurvey.co.uk/leisure.

Key to Symbols Used

Level of difficulty:

Easy 🐚

Fair 🐚 🐚

More challenging 🐚 🐚 🐚

Map symbols:

🚗 Park & start

── Tarred Road

── Unpaved road

- - - - - Footpath

■ Building

+ Church

▲ Triangulation pillar or
  other landmark

🪣 Pub

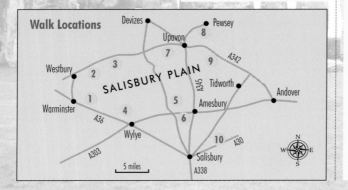

Walk Locations

Devizes • • Pewsey

Upavon 8

Westbury • 3 7

2 9 A342

SALISBURY PLAIN

A345 Tidworth

Warminster • 1 5 Amesbury Andover •

4 6

Wylye 10 A30

A36

A303 Salisbury •

5 miles A338

6

1 Battlesbury & Scratchbury

The escarpment, prehistory and the Army dominating a 7-mile circuit near Warminster

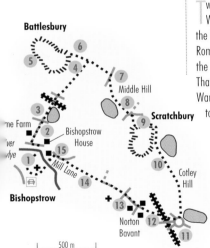

Battlesbury

6

5

4

7

Middle Hill

8

3

Scratchbury

9

2 Bishopstrow House

15

ne Farm

River Wylye

Mill Lane

1

10

Cotley Hill

14

Bishopstrow

13

12

Norton Bavant

11

500 m

Two of the best and biggest Wiltshire hill-forts, dating from the last days of the Iron Age before Roman conquest, look down from the chalk massif on all around them. That includes the School of Infantry at Warminster. Battlesbury still lives up to its name. A modern observation post on an ancient rampart looks into firing ranges across the rolling downland of Salisbury Plain. Scratchbury is softer in outline and position. Middle Hill, between them, is distinctive in its own way

Level: ♥
Length: 7 miles
Terrain: Gentle climbs and almost perfect paths with only a couple of arable fields.
Park & start: From **Church Lane** at **Bishopstrow** which is off the B3414.
Start ref: ST 895 437.
Postcode: BA12 9HN
Public transport: Trains to Warminster and buses from there to Wylye.
Websites: www.nortonbavant.co.uk
www.warminster.co.uk

for a single tree-covered prehistoric burial mound. This is an excellent introduction to the Plain.

Norton Bavant Church

1 Set off from the gateway of **St Aldhelm's Church**, beside the **Old Rectory**, along the cul-de-sac lane (N) into the meadows. Follow a leafy path which crosses the **River Wylye** and brings us to the main road in 500 metres.

2 Turn left along the pavement (W), away from **Bishopstrow House**, along the pavement beside **Old Stones**. In 125 metres we turn right (N) into the drive to **Home Farm**. This and the track that follows brings us to a cross-roads of paths in 600 metres.

3 Proceed straight ahead (NE), through or beside the wood, to the railway bridge which we cross in 400 metres. Also cross the military road in 150 metres. Follow the track beside the scrubby strip of grass. **Battlesbury Wood** and a series of strip lynchets are up to your left.

4 Turn left (NW) at the end of the penning in 800 metres. Now follow the fencing, beside the enclosure with the strip lynchets, up to the bigger earthworks of **Battlesbury** in 300 metres.

5 Walk around the hill-fort, which overlooks **Warminster Training Centre**, and come back to this kissing gate after a 1,500 metre circuit.

6 Return downhill (SE), to the end of the penning in 300 metres, and then continue straight ahead down the grassy strip between the fields on **Steps Down**. Descend

into the dip, in 400 metres, and drop down on to the military road.

7 Turn right, for 50 metres, and then left to climb up and over **Middle Hill**. Pass to the right of a conspicuous tree-topped burial mound and drop down to a small wood in 500 metres.

8 Keep the trees to your right and descend across strip lynchets to a junction of tracks in the dip in 250 metres. Continue straight

ahead along the road towards the farm for just 25 metres.

9 Turn right (S) and follow the fence up to the earthworks of **Scratchbury Camp** in 150 metres. The official line of the path bears left (E), along the rampart, which it follows

around the corner in 300 metres, for a further 300 metres (S) along the eastern side of the hill-fort.

10 Above the chestnuts and ashes of the semi-circular wood, **The Copse** we turn left on the other side of the fence-line and

Battlesbury from Scratchbury

Battlesbury hill-fort

cross the hilltop grain field diagonally (SE), and then the fence in the next field, to the top of the escarpment on **Cotley Hill** in 1,000 metres. Follow the terraced track (S) down the great grassy slope to gates to the right of the trees beside **Cotley Hill Roundabout** in 300 metres.

11 Cross the B3414 and turn right, towards Norton Bavant, to the railway bridge in 150 metres.

12 Cross the bridge and turn immediately right, down the steps, into the arable field. Head for the ash tree (NE), beside the gap on the other side, in 200 metres. Follow the hedgerow to the **Old Bakery** and then the lane to a junction in 300 metres.

13 Bear right, away from the houses of **Norton Bavant**, to the next junction, in 200 metres. **All Saints' Church** is to our left - with its crypt and inscriptions to the Benett family - and involves a diversion of 400 metres there and back. Return to here. Our onward path is straight ahead along the drive through the parkland. Cross the drive,

William Cobbett rode our walk on Friday 1 September 1826: 'There are two villages, one called Norton Bavant, and the other Bishopstrow, which I think form, together, one of the prettiest spots that my eyes ever beheld.'

which leads to **Norton Bavant Manor**, in 400 metres.

14 Enter the meadows, following the hedge which you keep to your left, and continue straight ahead across the next drive in 500 metres. Cross the fields to **Watery Lane** and the main road in 200 metres.

15 Continue along the B3414 - using the pavement - for 150 metres and then turn left (SW) into **Mill Lane**. Walk between the former industrial buildings and cross the leat and River Wylye over picturesque bridges. In 500 metres our path bends to the right (W), into the playing field, to bring us back to **St Aldhelm's Church** in 150 metres.

Bishopstrow Church

2 Westbury White Horse & Bratton

*Iconic symbol beside the site of a pivotal
battle that saved England*

Bratton Castle is another of Wiltshire's major Iron Age hill-forts. The famous White Horse is associated with the nearby Battle of Edington but more likely had earlier Celtic origins. The West of England mainline railway runs across the valley which is unusual in being a partially industrial setting. Reeves Agricultural Works manufactured farming equipment at Bratton until 1970. The 200-feet high chimney of Westbury Cement Works is a landmark to match the White Horse. Above them both, our route passes the quarry that produces chalk for concrete making, in what is still a working landscape.

Map showing route with numbered waypoints: Flowers Farm, Tiswell Spring, The Hollow, Port Way, White Horse, Bratton Castle, Lower Westbury Road, Fair View Farm, Newtown, Beggar's Knoll, chalk pit. Waypoints 1–8 marked. Scale 500 m.

Level: 🥾 🥾
Length: 5 miles
Terrain: A climb up the escarpment to return to the hilltop but otherwise nothing demanding.
Park & start: From the car-park above **Westbury White Horse**, which is reached by going up **Castle Road** from the B3098 in **Bratton** village.
Start ref: ST 900 514.
Postcode: BA13 4SP
Public transport: Trains to Westbury and from there to Market Lavington.
Websites: www.westburywiltshire.co.uk
wiltshirewhitehorses.org.uk

13

1 Set off into the English Heritage earthworks (N) of **Bratton Castle** in 75 metres. Inside the Iron Age banks and ditches we pass a well preserved Neolithic long barrow. Turn left (W) on reaching the escarpment in 200 metres.

Bratton Castle

Two white horses

2 Overlook the **White Horse** - at 755 feet above sea level - in 400 metres and then follow the Wessex Ridgeway beside the fence (SW) at the top edge of the steep slope. In 1,000 metres, on the hillside, we come to **Long River Road**.

3 Turn left (E), up the road, to the chalky five-way junction in 400 metres. Here we turn sharply right (SW), into the byway in front of the gate to **Lafarge Chalk Quarry**. We are now at 711 feet above sea level.

④ Also turn right (NW), into **Short River Road**, at the next junction of tracks in 500 metres. The hilltop plateau gives way to the main slope in 300 metres at **Beggar's Knoll**. Here we descend from the wooded escarpment into **Westbury** suburbia at **Newtown**. This brief urban experience is necessary to provide a circuit of paths.

⑤ Stop immediately after bungalow **No. 31** which is opposite **The Butts** in 750 metres. Here we turn right (NE) into an alleyway behind back gardens which then follows the cemetery wall down to **Bratton Road** in 500 metres.

Chestnut horses above Newtown

⑥ Turn right (E) and leave the town. Bear left at corner after **Fair View Farm**, in 400 metres, down and along a dirt road with the **Cement Works** to your left and the **White Horse** up to your right. Follow this track, which is the Mid Wilts Way, as it bends left and then right in 1,000 metres to become **Lower Westbury Road**. In a further 1,300 metres it brings us to a junction at **Flowers Farm**.

Iron Age ditch and ramparts

(7) Here we turn right (S), up **The Hollow**, and cross the main road in 200 metres. Follow the Wessex Ridgeway which climbs the slope to the **Port Way** in 600 metres.

(8) Turn right (SW), uphill, to re-enter **Bratton Castle**. In 250 metres we turn right (W) along the main rampart of the hill-fort and follow it around to the car-park in 700 metres.

The present Westbury White Horse was re-cut in 1778 over and around the sketchy outline of a much smaller Celtic-style horse that faced the other way.

Horse from the hill

3 **Edington & Tinhead**

*Battlefield vista above the priory built
to celebrate Alfred's famous victory*

I n size and style, Edington's parish church makes up for the virtual disappearance of the next-door priory. The place assumed its importance due to fighting hereabouts that secured the decisive victory of King Alfred's reign. That had its sequel in Danish submission on the Somerset Levels to Christianity at Aller and a peace treaty sealed at Wedmore. This walk explores a village and then ventures around a cliff-hanger of steep slopes with dramatic views.

Level:

Length: 5 miles

Terrain: Climbs up and down the escarpment but otherwise largely level on easy paths.

Park and start: In **Edington** village - reached by the B3098 - at the **Priory Church**.

Start ref: ST 926 533.

Postcode: BA13 4QH

Public transport: Buses from Westbury to Market Lavington.

Websites: www.edingtonfriends.org.uk
www.visionofbritain.org.uk

Present-day warfare will often be heard as noises off but none of these paths actually enters the firing ranges.

Lower Road

Edington

13

11

12

Manor Court

The Lamb

1 2

3

4

Coulston Hill

Salisbury Hollow

5

Luccombe Bottom

10

Picquet Hill

9

● reservoir

8 Edington Hill

Tottenham Wood

Tinhead Hill

Patcombe Hill

6

checkpoint ✗ 7

500 m

Edington Church

(1) Set off (E) along **Monastery Road** from the **Church of Blessed Virgin Mary, St Katharine, and All Saints**. This bring us to a corner in 150 metres where we follow the high wall around to the left.

(2) Now turn right, in 50 metres, and walk the length of **The Weir** to multiple junctions in 300 metres. Continue straight ahead through **Greenhills** for 100 metres to a triangle of grass beside No. 12. Here we go into an alley and emerge at **The Court** in 100 metres.

(3) Turn immediately right (S), beside another triangle of grass, and walk up a narrow footpath beside the duck pond to

Shepherd's Cottage and **The Lamb** public house in 200 metres.

(4) Turn left (E), along the main street, and then right in 125 metres. Enter **Long Hollow** but then turn immediately left, beside the **Old Chapel**, to begin the long climb up **Salisbury Hollow**. This soon becomes a deep-cut byway

through the trees. Proceed straight ahead at the first junction of tracks in 900 metres.

(5) Pass the turnpike milestone - Bath 17 miles, Sarum 19 - and then turn right (SW) at the next junction of flinty tracks on **Coulston Hill** in 400 metres. Walk the length of this wide, unfenced byway, with

Village duck pond

The Lamb

Salisbury Plain rolling away to your left. We are now on the 700 feet contour. **Tottenham Wood** is to your right as you go over the next rise in 800 metres, then a barn to the left on **Tinhead Hill** in 400 metres, followed by a junction in 350 metres.

6 Turn left here (S) to the warning signs in 200 metres. Here we turn right (W) and keep the **Military Firing Range** to our left. Descend to **Checkpoint V6** in the valley in 1,200 metres.

7 Turn immediately right (N) as you approach it. Follow the grass track rather than the road. In 400 metres this forks and we bear left through a gate and continue straight ahead up and over **Patcombe Hill**. Continue straight ahead at a junction of tracks in 800 metres.

Alfred, King of Wessex, saved England from Danish conquest at the decisive Battle of Edington in May 876.

Follow the fence

8 Approach the reservoir on **Edington Hill** in 300 metres and go through the gate to the left of it.

9 We now have a panoramic view towards Westbury and Trowbridge from the escarpment of **Picquet Hill**. Follow the sloping terrace (NW) around **Luccombe Bottom**. This becomes a hollow way as it curves round and down, beside a much larger reservoir, into leafy **Sandy Lane** in 750 metres.

Where we turn away

(10) Follow this (N) to **Westbury Road** in 350 metres. Here we turn left for 35 metres, into the layby, and then cross to the gate beside the village sign.

(11) Turn right in this arable field, following the hedgerow along the to the first corner in 150 metres and then the second corner in a further 200 metres. Here we drop down to a kissing gate and cross the pasture (NE) to the roadside gate in 50 metres.

(12) Turn left (N), to pass **Manor Court**, down **Greater Lane** to the junction in 75 metres.

(13) Turn right (E), along **Lower Road**, into the village. Fork left in 250 metres. Turn left in 50 metres, into **Inmead** and then right in a further 50 metres, opposite **The Grange**. The picturesque path through the gate returns us to the **Priory Church** in 175 metres.

As 'Ethandun', Edington was left by Alfred to his wife, and remained a royal possession, with King Edgar granting it to Romsey Abbey in 968.

When William Cobbett rode through Edington in 1826, it was glowing with walnuts, apples and pears, and in a park-pond 'I saw what I never saw before; namely, some black swans'.

21

Luccombe Bottom

4 **Chitterne & Knook**

*Bronze Age barrows and Iron Age settlements
in an 8-mile route from a typical Plain village*

Typical Salisbury Plain village and countryside with just a taste of being on the edge of the military ranges. You begin to feel the vast-ness of a landscape composed of the compressed shells of countless billion miniature creatures from a warm-water sea which has itself floated on the globe's magma. It was elevated by continental plate tectonics as Africa slid into Europe. Chalk is the ideal filter for clear-water streams. The result for us is rolling downland that is the essence of Salisbury Plain. It is also up to a standard normal for Wiltshire in terms of prehistoric monuments.

Level: 🐾
Length: 8 miles
Terrain: Ordinary decent countryside without anything exceptional or demanding.
Park and start: In the vicinity of **All Saints' and St Mary's Church** in **Chitterne** which is on the B390.
Start ref: ST 992 440.
Postcode: BA12 0LJ
Public transport: None.
Websites: www.chitterne.com
www.wiltshire.gov.uk

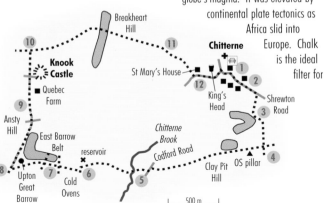

(1) Set off (S) towards the main road, which is **Bidden Lane**, in 150 metres. Turn left (SE) along it and head uphill out of the village. This is **Shrewton Road**.

(2) In 600 metres we leave the village. Continue uphill for 350 metres and then turn right (S) into the big arable field. A bridleway heads up the slope to the left-hand end of the shelter belts in 300 metres.

(3) Bear left (SE) on the other side of the fence and follow it to the end of the field in 700 metres.

(4) Turn right (W) at this cross-roads of tracks. Pass an Ordnance Survey triangulation pillar (at 580 feet above sea level) in 250 metres. Keep the copse to your right in another 250 metres. We begin the descent from **Clay Pit Hill**, keeping the parish boundary hedgerow to our left for 800 metres, and then to the right, as we drop down the middle of a dry combe to **Codford Road** in a further 800 metres.

(5) Turn left, up the road, and then right in 100 metres into the field. Cross **Chitterne Brook** and walk up to the bridleway gate to the right of the dense hedgerow in 400 metres. Enter the field beyond the trees in 200 metres and continue straight ahead to the corner in 300

Walking the dogs

Quebec Farm

metres where we cross to the other side of the hedgerow.

Follow the hedge to a hilltop reservoir which is beside the next track in 900 metres. Turn left and then right to cross this path. The next

section of our route, between **Cold Ovens** and **The Ruins**, brings us to woods where we cross another track in 500 metres.

Follow **East Barrow Belt**, which we keep to our right,

and pass its Bronze Age burial mound which is **Upton Great Barrow**, in 300 metres.

In 100 metres we come to a green lane which runs across the top of the escarpment overlooking Knook at 440 feet above sea level. Turn right (NE) along the track. Proceed into the dip, beside **North Barrow Belt**, and cross the main road on **Ansty Hill** in 1,000 metres.

> 'The Chitterne Flock' of Hampshire Down sheep – farmer Joseph Dean's pride and joy – featured in the Farmer and Stock Breeder of 24 July 1905.

Upton Great Barrow, a ten feet high bell-shaped mound covering a Wessex Culture cremation from the Bronze Age, may have been the 'Golden Barrow' source of amber, faience and gold beads and other ornaments on show in Devizes Museum.

9 The Army road (N) on the other side is a public right of way. It passes **Quebec Farm** and brings us to a **Private Military Road** in 900 metres. Turn left and then immediately right to cross this road. Follow the byway signs. You are allowed to proceed across it here. On the other side, the earthworks of **Knook Castle** Iron Age settlement

are to our right, and a beech plantation to the left.

10 In 500 metres we reach a water tank and turn right (E) into a green lane which doubles as the Imber perimeter path. This leads us into rolling scenery with the **Military Firing Range** to our left.

In 1,400 metres the track goes over **Breakheart Hill** and passes through a shelter belt.

11 Follow the byway (SE) down into **Chitterne** village in 2,000 metres. The track emerges through trees on to the main road beside **St Mary's House**.

To Breakheart Hill

12 Turn left, to the **King's Head** in 250 metres. Beyond it, in 100 metres, we turn left into **St Mary's Close** and then immediately right into the playing field. Cross this to return to the church tower, through gate piers, in 200 metres.

The King's Head

St Mary's Close

5 Bustard Inn & Netheravon

*Across the Ranges, when the firing schedule permits,
through 8 miles of long grass otherwise reserved
for the great bustard*

This is a magical walk, almost entirely on gritty tracks, through the endless long grass of the Larkhill Ranges. Access is allowed along these public paths when hazardous military activity is not taking place. That is usually the case at weekends and during block leave periods at Easter, during August, and for Christmas. It samples one of the biggest open landscapes in Europe, where about the only fence is an occasional compound for stock penning or some military purpose. This includes aircraft instrument checking and the area is also used as an aerial dropping zone for men and materials. Other markers, such as white posts with star signs, often signify ancient monuments.

Level:

Length: 8 miles

Terrain: Wild country, but well-defined tracks, with no real slopes, and not even a stile to climb or a gate to open.

Park and start: As a customer of the **Bustard Inn** which is the next building beyond **Rollestone Camp**, off the B3086 between **Shrewton** and **Larkhill**.

Start ref: SU 091 461.

Postcode: SP3 4DU

Public transport: Bus to Rollestone Camp between Shrewton and Amesbury.

Websites: www.durringtonwilts.co.uk
www.greatbustard.com

Wexland Farm

Gun and Dog

Newfoundland Farm Wood

Netheravon

Blackball Firs

Netheravon Down

Robin Hood's Ball

Alton Down

Bustard Inn

500 m

① Set off into the **Military Ranges**, where it is safe to proceed along public rights of way provided the red danger flags are not flying, beside the old VP9 at **Bustard Vedette** in 75 metres.

Observe signs

Safe to proceed

② Also go straight ahead (N) beside current VP9 **Bustard Checkpoint** in a further 400 metres.

③ Beyond, in 200 metres, we turn right (NE) at the end of the pine trees. Pass to the right of the next plantation in 100 metres. Our track, grassy and rutted, is to the left of the military road signed for QinetiQ at OP3.

④ We are heading for the central line of woods at **Blackball Firs**. In 600 metres our rough track - which is a public byway - joins a military road and turns left along it. In 200 metres we pass through the trees, keeping beech directly on the left and pines to the right. Ours is the left-hand of two roads through the wood.

(5) As we emerge from the trees, in 600 metres, we enter the open country of an aerial dropping zone designated **Area 11**. Head towards distant encampments above Netheravon, with a Royal Aircraft Establishment compound up the slope to the left. Also to the left are the beeches and pines of

The great bustard - Europe's largest land bird - was shot out of existence in Britain in the 19th century, but has now been reintroduced to Salisbury Plain from Hungary, via pens at Tilshead.

Eastwards, bearing left

Newfoundland Farm Wood which we pass in 900 metres. The next feature, signified by star signs to the left, is a Bronze Age burial mound in 200 metres.

(6) Hereon, for 1,500 metres, there are pine trees to the left and the open grassland of **Netheravon Down** to the right. Then, for 300 metres, there are trees up the slopes

on each side. Next we are back in open country and follow the valley bottom track up and over a ramped road in 750 metres.

(7) We are now walking (E) down into ordinary agricultural countryside, beside **Wexland Farm** in 750 metres, to a cross-roads at the edge of the ranges. From here,

Blackball Firs

if you wish, you can continue to the **Gun and Dog Inn**, 750 metres away in **Netheravon** village.

(8) Our onward route from the cross-roads below Wexland Farm returns to the ranges. Face the village and turn right (SW) to walk up the slope with your back to the farm.

The Royal School of Artillery grew out of a practice camp at the outbreak of the South African War in 1899, with permanent buildings following for the Great War in 1914, and the present barracks in 1937.

(9) On the hilltop in 800 metres we fork right and then continue straight ahead at the cross-roads along a gritty track down into the wooded valley beside **Netheravon Down**. Continue straight ahead in 1,500 metres as you rise into a prehistoric landscape, first of Celtic fields, and then earlier Neolithic long barrows and a causewayed camp from 3500 BC.

(10) This long road takes us through pine woods to a major junction beside the stock penning of **Robin Hood's Ball** in a further 2,500 metres.

(11) Here we turn right (ENE), beside the almost invisible earthworks in the stock pen-ning. Bear left at a three-way split of

Between 1897 and 1902, the War Department acquired 43,000 acres from Market Lavington to Larkhill - much of it at the current price for best farmland, which was £10 per acre.

The western ranges across to Imber and Warminster were bought for by the military between 1928 and 1932.

Off-roading on Netheravon Down

Road open

trackways on the brow of the hill and then in 75 metres continue straight ahead into a grassy hollow. This descends to the left-hand side of **Bustard Wood** in 500 metres.

(12) From here you head for the chimneys and distinctive Scots pines of the **Bustard Inn**. In 200 metres we emerge from the long grass beside an electricity sub station and the side wall of **Bustard Cottages**.

Robin Hood's Ball

6 Normanton & Stonehenge

Around the World Heritage Site in the classic circuit of British archaeology

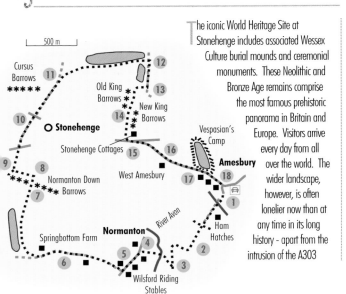

The iconic World Heritage Site at Stonehenge includes associated Wessex Culture burial mounds and ceremonial monuments. These Neolithic and Bronze Age remains comprise the most famous prehistoric panorama in Britain and Europe. Visitors arrive every day from all over the world. The wider landscape, however, is often lonelier now than at any time in its long history - apart from the intrusion of the A303

Level: 💚
Length: 8 miles
Terrain: Easy paths, well marked, with no serious hills.
Park and start: In **Amesbury** where we turn off **Stonehenge Road** - beside **Little Thatch** - into **Recreation Road**, to a car-park beside playing fields in 150 metres.
Start ref: SU 150 412.
Postcode: SP4 7BA
Public transport: Buses between Salisbury and Pewsey.
Websites: www.this-is-amesbury.co.uk
www.stonehenge.co.uk

trunk road. That we have to cross, a couple of times, but can otherwise escape from. The other flow, bridged twice, is the idyllic River Avon.

1 Set off from the entrance to the car-park by turning left into a path on the other side of the fence. This leads (SW) to **Ham Hatches**, where we cross the **River Avon**, in 200 metres. Bear left and then right to pass the side-wall of the semi-detached farm cottages.

2 Follow the farm track towards Durnford, going up and over the hill in 500 metres. Proceed straight ahead from the cross-roads of tracks on top, down to the gates in 400 metres. Turn right (NW) through the smallest of them and follow the hedgerow to the chalkpit in 150 metres.

3 Turn left beside it (S) along a cattle track beside scrubby marshland. In 300 metres we turn right and cross a wooden bridge. This boggy path (NW) through the poplars leads to a bridge over the **River Avon**, in 200 metres, followed by smaller brick bridge over a secondary flow.

4 Keep the garden and then a thatched wall to your left. Bear right in the corner of the pasture, in 150 metres, and go through the kissing gate. A grassy strip beside the avenue brings us to a roadside postbox in 200 metres.

5 Turn left (SW) and follow the road through **Normanton** hamlet to **Wilsford Racing Stables** in 500 metres. Proceed for a further 75 metres, and then turn right (W) between the thatched cottages into

River Avon

the drive to **Springbottom Farm**. There is an idyllic path through the roadside trees.

6 Pass the grain store on the hill in 800 metres. In **Springbottom**, in a further 800 metres, we follow the drive around to the left of the buildings and barns. Beyond we continue straight ahead for 100 metres and then bear right (N), away from a dirt track and the power cables, into a wide grassy strip between the paddocks.

(7) This gradually climbs on to the skyline where we pass between the Bronze Age burial mounds on **Normanton Down** in 1,500 metres.

(8) Pass the **Stonehenge Estate** sign and turn left (W) in 100 metres into National Trust land. Follow the fence to the next

Normanton Down

Leaving Springbottom

track in 350 metres. **Bush Barrow**, famous for its finds, can be still be identified from its scrubby elders.

(9) Turn right along this byway (NE) and cross the A303 in 500 metres.

(10) Continue straight ahead and pass **Stonehenge** in 700 metres. Also cross this road, near the access point to the monument, and proceed straight ahead. The track passes to the right of the **Cursus Barrows** and then crosses slight

Stonehenge

traces of the **Cursus** ceremonial way as the road bends to the left (N) in 800 metres.

(11) Here we turn right and (E) and follow the north bank of the Cursus beside the belt of trees. **Larkhill Camp** is to our left. In 1,400 metres we leave come to the end of the Cursus and pass its notice board.

Though as enigmatic as ever, Stonehenge performs as a physical calendar for showing the turning points of the sun at midsummer (days shorten) and midwinter (days lengthen) plus phases of the moon.

New King Barrows

(12) Turn right (S) along the track beside another belt of trees. We pass residual remains of a long barrow burial mound which flanked contemporary access points to the Cursus.

(13) In 350 metres, at the end of the trees, we pass the first of the Bronze Age **Old King Barrows**.

Turn right (W) to pass the second barrow in 150 metres. Turn left (N) in another 150 metres, after the third barrow. We are now on **King Barrows Ridge** which looks down across **Stonehenge Down**.

(14) The impressive line of **New King Barrows** and their

accompanying beech trees bring us to a gate on to the A303 verge in 900 metres.

(15) Turn left and then right, beside thatched **Stonehenge Cottages**, to cross the main road in two stages. On the other side we turn left (E).

(16) In 250 metres the pavement bends to the right (SE) beside what becomes a slip road. Spot the

Stonehenge Cottages

All the Stones of Stonehenge were brought for afar, with the smaller bluestones from sacred Preseli Mountain in Wales, and bigger sarsen stones from Wiltshire's Marlborough Downs.

distance from London on a 1767-dated turnpike milestone. This is **Stonehenge Road**.

(17) Continue along the pavement through **West Amesbury** in 600 metres. In a further 600 metres we pass Iron Age **Vespasian's Camp**

but its earthworks are totally hidden in trees on the other side of the road

(18) Proceed to the corner beside **Little Thatch** in 400 metres. Here we turn right, up **Recreation Road**, to return to the playing field in 150 metres.

7 Marden & Chirton

*From ancient Marden to the keep-out edge
of the Impact Area and back via Norman Chirton*

Two churches with Norman treasures and a contemporary lost village give a mediaeval feel to the start and finish. There is also industrial archaeology at Marden Mill though its iron wheel has ceased to grind animal feed. An excellent public house (please take off muddy shoes) adds to the civilised ambience. On the other side of the walk, up on the slopes, we stroll beside the edge of the impact area of the artillery ranges and look across wide open spaces towards the lost village of Imber.

Level: 🐾 🐾
Length: 6 miles
Terrain: Variety of paths, mainly grassy or gritty, but occasionally arable, and climbs up and down the escarpment.
Park and start: As a customer of **The Millstream** public house at **Marden** which is reached from the A342.
Start ref: SU 087 579.
Postcode: SN10 3RQ
Public transport: Buses from Devizes to Pewsey.
Websites: www.chirton.org
www.visionofbritain.org.uk

The walk starts (and therefore finishes) at the Millstream hostelry in Marden. Say no more, apart from nice.

500 m

1. Set off uphill into the village along **The Street** (SW) and pass **All Saint's Church** in 200 metres. In a further 150 metres, after the **Village Hall**, we turn left (E) between the beech hedge of **Chequers** and thatched wall of **Orchard Cottage**.

2. This picturesque path leads into the meadows in 100 metres. Bear right for 75 metres to the stile beside the ditch. Follow it to

The Norman doorway and fine chancel arch in All Saints' Church at Marden date from before 1120, during Bishop Roger's episcopacy at Salisbury.

Marden church porch

the kissing gate at the other end of the field in 250 metres. Go straight ahead across the next pasture to an arable field in 100 metres. Cross this to the grassy bank in 250 metres.

3. Here, on an ancient causeway which forms the parish boundary, we turn right (S). Follow this elevated green lane towards the main road and the nearest hills.

4. Having crossed the **A342**, in 1,000 metres, the raised track passes **Hinderway Plantation** in 700 metres.

5. Now turn right, on the grassy hillside, and pass the Iron Age earthworks of **Broadbury Banks** which stretch to our left in 300 metres. Beyond the trees, in 250 metres, we follow the fence straight ahead. Keep it to your right as you walk along the side of an arable field (SW) to the edge of the military **Impact Area** in 800 metres.

Arable hinterland

6 Turn right (W) along the rough road beside the red flag. **The Ridgeway** doubles as the White Horse Trail. Proceed straight ahead through the next belt of trees in 600 metres. In a further 1,000 metres, beside a red flag on an otherwise featureless plateau called **Chirton Maggot**.

7 Here we turn right (N). Ignore 'Private Land' signs (intended to keep out squaddies rather than walkers). A public bridleway follows the grass strip which we keep to our left. At the end of the grain field, in 500 metres, you bear left (NW), down a grassy hollow way.

Opposite All Saints' Church, beside meadows where we walk, is the site of the first Marden village which is thought to have been wiped out by the plague.

Broadbury Banks

Beside the Impact Area

8 Turn right (N) at the junction of grass tracks at the bottom of the escarpment in 200 metres. Also bear right (NW) at the following junction, in 200 metres, and then the third, in 700 metres. We are heading towards the distant White Horse - above Alton

Barnes - and the much closer main road.

9 Cross the **Andover Road** in 250 metres to a grassy path (N) which follows the right-hand side of the trees. It brings us to **Small Street** in 500 metres.

10 Turn left (W) into **Chirton** village. Turn right (N) on reaching **The Street** in 300 metres. Signed towards Patney, this passes **Manor Farm**. The road bends to the right (E) beside the **Church of St John the Baptist** in 500 metres.

11 At the following corner, beside the appropriately

'Imber on the down, four miles from any town,' was the motto of the village at the heart of the ranges which was evacuated on the order of Churchill's War Cabinet in December 1943 to train troops for the forthcoming invasion of Europe.

Ridgeway rider

12 Turn left (N) into another green lane. In 300 metres, at a stile immediately before a field entrance, we turn right (E) and follow the fence along a grassy strip between two arable fields.

13 In 600 metres we approach **Marden Mill**. Descend to the drive beside **Mill Cottage** and turn right to return to **The Millstream** in 150 metres.

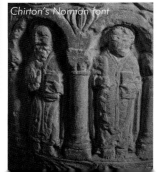

Chirton's Norman font

named **Corner House** in 150 metres, we continue straight ahead into a double-hedged farm track.

This takes us into the meadows and brings us to a junction of paths in 700 metres.

On manoeuvres

8 Fyfield & Pewsey

One white horse looks across to another over the Vale of Pewsey and its canal

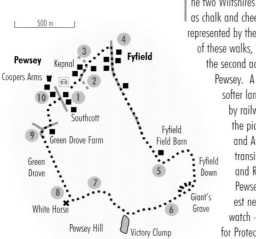

The two Wiltshires are as different as chalk and cheese. The first, represented by the Salisbury Plain of these walks, looks towards the second across the Vale of Pewsey. A rich and fertile softer landscape is crossed by railways, roads and the picturesque Kennet and Avon Canal in transit between Bath and Reading.

Pewsey claims the oldest neighbourhood watch — 'An Association for Protection of Persons and Property and the Prosecution and Punishment of Felons and Other Offenders' — formed in 1825.

Level: 🐾 🐾
Length: 6 miles
Terrain: Flat on the bottom and on the top but with an escarpment between.
Park and start: As a customer of the **Coopers Arms** in **Ball Road** at **Pewsey**.
Start ref: SU 168 599.
Postcode: SN9 5BL
Public transport: Buses from Devizes, Marlborough and Salisbury.
Websites: www.pewsey-uk.co.uk
www.wiltshirewhitehorses.org.uk

8

Fyfield & Pewsey

47

(1) Set off down the lane (S) into **Southcott**, to **No. 2 Willow Reach**, in 150 metres. Here we turn left (E), up the drive to **Down View** and then continue straight ahead at the corner in 30 metres. Cross the arable field. Continue straight ahead from the corner of the field, over a stile, and cross a pasture.

(2) In 400 metres we come to a green lane and turn left along it (N), into **Kepnal** hamlet in 75 metres, and follow the track to the right and then left, as it turns into an access road.

(3) Turn right (NE) in 200 metres, immediately after the right-hand cottage, to the next road in a further 200 metres.

Coopers Arms

(4) Turn right (S), in **Fyfield** hamlet, straight ahead along the road through **Fyfield Farm** which becomes a green lane and brings us to **Fyfield Farm Barn** in 1,800 metres. Proceed straight ahead to the foot of the escarpment in 150 metres.

(5) The track now bends to the left (NE) to become an ancient hollow way to the flat-topped

summit of **Fyfield Down** in 750 metres. Here we keep the fence to our left and cross the banks and platforms of an Iron Age field system, to reach (S) the bigger and earlier earthwork of Neolithic **Giant's Grave** in 500 metres.

(6) Follow the fence, keeping it to the left, as we take advantage of a continuous ribbon of open country that follows (SW) the

The Giant's Grave is a Neolithic long barrow, 315 feet in length and 7 feet high with side ditches, which was built over a mortuary chamber of disaritculated bones dating from 3500 BC.

Fyfield Down

chalk escarpment overlooking Pewsey. Cross the stile in 400 metres, into the next pasture, and pass to the right of **Victory Clump** on **Pewsey Hill** in 700 metres.

(7) Follow the hillside track (NW) to the far end of this pasture in 600 metres. Again cross into the next pasture. We are heading (W) to a fenced enclosure towards the top of

the slope in 600 metres. This surrounds the **Pewsey White Horse**.

Hollow way

Pewsey Hill

Giant's Grave

10 Turn right (E), keeping the houses to your left, to the lane between **King's Corner** and **Southcott** in 300 metres. Turn left (N) along **Southcott Lane**, into Pewsey, to **Coopers Arms** in 400 metres.

King Alfred

8 Head directly downhill (N) towards Pewsey and follow the long tongue of grassland, appropriately known as **Green Drove**, which becomes a tarred road in 1,200 metres.

9 Turn right (NE), along the road to **Green Drove Farm** in 200 metres. Turn left (N) beside barns, along a footpath to the trees and **Swan Meadow** in 350 metres.

Green Drove

9 Everleigh & Baden Down

*The great emptiness of the northern plain,
entirely part of the military estate*

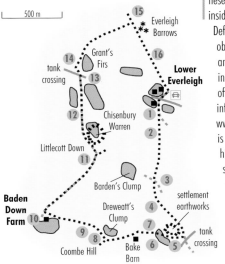

These rights of way are entirely inside and across Ministry of Defence land so you must observe the bylaws generally and all notices and warnings in particular. Before setting off, check for specific information on www.access.mod.uk. This is a big landscape of low hills and long valleys that seem as wide as the elastic will stretch. Sameness soon becomes the norm. Antiquarian researcher Richard Fenton

Level:

Length: 7 miles

Terrain: Easy tracks and nothing much to climb.

Park and start: In the side road beside the cottages at **Lower Everleigh** which is on the **A342** in the dip between **Upavon Airfield** and **Everleigh** hamlet.

Start ref: SU 189 546.

Postcode: SN8 3HE

Public transport: Buses between Andover and Devizes.

Websites: www.everleigh.org.uk
www.wiltshire.gov.uk

excavated one of the barrows in 1805, during his *Tour in Quest of Genealogy.*

1 Set off (S) to the postbox and main road in 200 metres. Turn right (W) and then left (S) in 100 metres along the drive beside **Lower Everleigh Farm** which continues straight ahead as a byway.

2 In 350 metres we fork right, off the main track, along a rutted grassy path between hawthorn bushes, up and over the rise, into open grassland. We are heading towards a communications mast of the far distant skyline with a military road down in the valley to our left.

3 Continue straight ahead at a cross-roads of military tracks in 1,300 metres. In 500 metres we continue straight ahead at a junction of tracks.

Lower Everleigh Farmhouse

4 Ours bends to the left (SE) between featureless grass-lands though you may spot cars on a road ahead. On approaching **Tank Crossing W** in 900 metres we turn right (W) and keep the star signed stock penning of an Iron Age settlement to our right.

5 In 300 metres we turn right, up through the long grass, to a bridleway gate, and bear left across the pasture to the next gate in the middle of the fence beside the trees, in 150 metres.

6 Turn right (NW) to the end of the shelter belt in 100 metres.

Iron Age settlement

7 Now turn left (W) to the next clumps of trees in 150 metres. Pass between them, keeping the first trees to your left, and then **Bake Barn** to the left in 250 metres. Follow its access track. We

A total of 42,000 acres of the Salisbury Plain military holdings are classified as a 'schedule three wilderness area'.

pass more Iron Age fields in stock penning to the right and continue beside the trees to the far end of the plantation on **Coombe Hill** in 500 metres.

8 Here we turn right (NW), beside a lump of concrete, into the final track through the wood. On the other side, in 300 metres, we come to a circle of mature beech trees known as **Dreweatt's Clump**.

9 Turn left (W), straight ahead into the grassland, towards a point to the left of Upavon Airfield. There are a pair of Bronze Age burial mounds to our left and another big barrow down to the right. As buildings and a wood become visible in the combe we descend towards them. Join the access road beside **Baden Down Farm** in 900 metres.

(10) Turn right (NE) beyond the buildings, in 150 metres, and follow the road up the valley beside **Littlecott Down**.

(11) In 1,600 metres we turn left (NW) towards the top of the valley and pass the star signs of an

Crimean War veteran and sporting baronet Sir John Astley (1828-94) of Everleigh, renowned as 'one of the finest judges of horseflesh in England', published memoirs entitled Fifty Years in the World of Sport at Home and Abroad.

Iron Age settlement followed by the scrubby enclosure of **Chisenbury Warren,** both across to our right.

(12) The track gradually bends towards the hilltop trees (N) in 1,200 metres. Here the bridleway passes to the left of the older beech wood but to the right of younger trees.

Bake Barn fir

Coombe Hill pines

keeping fields to your left and wild land to the right.

15 In 1,100 metres we come to a junction beside the magnificently preserved **Everleigh Barrows**.

16 Turn right (SW), along the ancient green lane which gradually descends across **West Everleigh Down** to the paddocks, fields and trees of **Lower Everleigh** hamlet in 1,800 metres.

13 In 300 metres we reach the road at the yellow-topped black markers of **Tank Crossing II**. Cross to the verge on the other side of the **A342** and then turn left (W) along it for 150 metres.

14 Now turn right (NE), along a byway, with arable fields to your left and the long grass and pine trees to your right. The track passes through **Grant's Firs** in 500 metres. Continue straight ahead,

Longstreet Down barrows

Returning to Lower Everleigh

10 Winterbournes & Figsbury

Clear chalk stream, grassy prehistoric hill-fort and deserted Roman road

This Wiltshire Winterbourne was the river of Isaak Walton of Compleat Angler fame when he was vicar of nearby Boscombe. That is now of note for the country's major military aviation test-base, across the valley from the micro-biological research station on Porton Down, with our side of the security fence having open access to a splendid hill-fort at Figsbury Ring and a grassy length of otherwise redundant Roman road. Many of the hedgerows are a kaleidoscope of colours and species including juniper - with gin-flavour berries - guelder rose, dogwood and spindle.

Level: 🥾

Length: 6 miles

Terrain: Well-marked paths and gentle slopes.

Park and start: From **Sherfield** car-park beside the **Winterbourne Arms** on the **A338** in **Winterbourne Dauntsey** village.

Start ref: SU 176 347.

Postcode: SP4 6EW

Public transport: Buses from Salisbury to Tidworth.

Websites: www.nationaltrust.org.uk
www.visionofbritain.org.uk

Winterbourne Arms

⑭

⑮ **Winterbourne Dauntsey**

Great Drove ⑬

⑫

①

②

Figsbury Ring

⑩ Hurdcott

③

④ Longacre

⑪

⑤

⑥

River Bourne

⑨

⑧

⑦

Roman road   Hillview Farm

500 m

1. Set off across the road (S) to **Paddock Close** in 100 metres. Turn right beside **No. 8** to **St Michael's Church** in 150 metres.

2. Turn left (SE), up **Figsbury Lane** for 250 metres. Go under the railway bridge (Waterloo-Exeter line) and continue straight ahead into the green lane on the other side. Walk up between the fields to the earthworks on top of the hill in 1,500 metres.

Figsbury: outer bank

Juniper berries

3. Here we enter National Trust land and bear left (E) across **Figsbury Rings** and its downland to the opposite corner in 500 metres. We are at 478 feet above sea level. Defence establishments at Boscombe Down and Porton Down are across to our left and the spire of Salisbury Cathedral - 404 feet high - rises to the right.

4. From the far corner we follow the access track (SE) down to the main road at **Longacre** and **Paddock House Farm** in 600 metres.

Roman road

5 Turn left (E) at the bus stop, along the grass verge, for 175 metres. Now cross the **A30** to the double-hedged bridleway on the other side (S). On reaching the trees in 300 metres we turn left (SE) and pass the communication mast.

6 In 250 metres, on approaching **Hillview Farm**, we turn right (E) and join a long grassy bank that stretches across the valley. This is the causeway of the Roman road from London to Exeter.

7 Cross the tarred road in 1,000 metres and proceed straight across the field to the trees in a further 400 metres. Here we cross the **A30** at the junction, into Old Malthouse Road.

8 Then turn right (NE) immediately after the gates in 30 metres. This bridleway descends through the scrub as a ancient double-hedged track. Pass a farmyard in 1,000 metres. Continue along the track and go under the railway bridge in 400 metres.

9 Next, in 175 metres, we cross the **A338**, into **Hurdcott Lane**. Pass the junction with **Black Horse Lane** in 225 metres.

The unusual thing above Figsbury Rings is that it has a deep inner ditch - well inside the main defences - which was dug to provide chalk for heightening the main bank in the 3rd century BC.

10 Turn left (SW) at **The Poplars** in 75 metres and pass **Watergate House**. Cross the **River Bourne** in 150 metres and then continue straight ahead (W) at the junction of tracks both in 75 metres and beside the **Sewage Works** entrance in another 75 metres.

11 Then in a further 50 metres we turn right (NE), through a kissing gate. Hereon we keep fields to the left and scrubby meadows to the right. Proceed straight ahead along the drive from **Hurdcott Farm** in 400 metres. Also go straight ahead as the main track bends to the right in 100 metres with **Home Bridge** to your right (don't cross it).

Twenty-year-old Sergeant Pilot George William Jefferys from this valley, buried in St Michael's churchyard, was shot down in a Hurricane over Clacton at the height of the Battle of Britain and died when his parachute failed to open, on 15 September 1940.

12 In 200 metres we come to a wide ford and turn left (NW) into **Great Drove**. In 75 metres we turn right (NE) through a kissing gate in the hedge

13 Once again you keep fields to the left and the scrubby meadows to the right. Proceed straight ahead for 600 metres to the tarred road.

14 Turn right (SE) to the footbridge beside the ford at **Riverside** in 200 metres. **Gaters Lane** takes us through **Winterbourne Gunner** hamlet to thatched **Peacock Cottage** - with matching topiary - in 200 metres.

15 Turn right beside the **Post Office**, along the pavement, to return to the **Winterbourne Arms** in 150 metres.

Great Drove ford

Footbridge at Riverside

Peacock Cottage topiary